HUNTING DOGS
ON THE JOB

BY ALLAN MOREY

The Child's World®
childsworld.com

Published by The Child's World®
1980 Lookout Drive • Mankato, MN 56003-1705
800-599-READ • www.childsworld.com

Photographs ©: Joe Michl/iStockphoto, cover, 1, 9; m01229 CC2.0, 5; iStockphoto, 6, 18, 20; Rebecca Ashworth/Shutterstock Images, 10; Action Sports Photography/Shutterstock Images, 13; Renee V CC2.0, 14; Craig Fritz/The New Mexican/AP Images, 15; Ingram Publishing/Newscom, 17

ISBN 9781503816121

LCCN 2016945608

Printed in the United States of America
PA02318

TABLE OF CONTENTS

FAST FACTS

The Job

- Dogs help people hunt many types of **game**.
- Bird dogs, or gun dogs, are the most common type of hunting dogs. They are divided into three main groups: **pointers**, **flushers**, and **retrievers**.
- Pointers help hunters find game.
- Flushers chase game from hiding spots.
- Retrievers bring back game that has been shot.

Training Time

- Hunting dogs often start **obedience** training at eight weeks old.
- Some dogs are ready to go on a hunt after several months of training. But it takes years of hunting for dogs to become great hunting dogs.

Common Breeds

- Pointing breeds include Brittanys, German shorthaired pointers, and English setters.
- Spaniels make good flushing dogs.
- Chesapeake Bay, Labrador, and golden retrievers are common retrieval dogs.

Upland Game Birds

- Upland game birds include pheasants, grouse, quail, and other nonwater game birds.
- These birds hide on the ground. Hunters need dogs to help find birds, flush them from their hiding spots, and then retrieve them after they have been shot.

Water Game Birds

- Water game birds include waterfowl, such as ducks and geese.
- Hunters shoot these game birds as they fly over wetland areas. Hunting dogs help hunters retrieve the birds from the water.

Chapter 1

IN THE FIELD

A pickup rumbled to a stop at the end of a dirt road. Two hunters stepped out of the truck. Around them, a field of dried prairie grasses spread out in every direction. It was the perfect spot to hunt pheasants.

The hunters wore tan pants and shirts to match their surroundings. They also wore orange hats and vests. The bright clothing was for safety. It would help any other hunters spot them.

Two crates sat in the bed of the truck. The hunters opened the crates. Two Brittanys with wavy white fur and reddish spots leaped out. The dogs ran around the pickup excitedly. "Heel!" shouted one of the hunters.

◀ **Brittanys are energetic, easy-to-train hunting dogs.**

The dogs quickly returned to the back of the truck, waiting for instructions.

Soon the hunters headed out into the field. The dogs trotted along with them. After the group was safely away from the road, one hunter called out, "Hunt!"

The dogs leaped into action. With noses pointed down, they wound back and forth through the field. As they ranged outward, the dogs always stayed within sight of the hunters. The landscape all around seemed the same to the hunters but not to the dogs. Their noses picked out different scents. They worked to sniff out where pheasants were hiding.

Suddenly one of the dogs stopped. It raised one of its front paws. Its snout pointed toward a clump of tall grass. It silently glanced from the grass to the hunter.

The hunters looked at each other. They both raised their guns to their shoulders. One hunter faced the left side of the field. The other faced to the right.

The hunter on the right walked slowly forward. The hunter approached the spot where the dog was pointing. Any second, a pheasant could burst from its cover.

▲ **Dogs such as the German shorthaired pointer have been bred to point at game.**

Chapter 2

LEARNING TO HUNT

Hunting dogs start training at a young age. A hunter **weans** a young hunting dog from its mother at approximately eight weeks. The puppy's obedience training begins shortly after.

First the hunter gets the puppy used to being crated. Crates help with potty training. But they are also important when traveling. The hunter might drive a long way to a hunting site. Putting hunting dogs in crates is the safest way for them to travel.

The hunter also teaches the puppy basic commands. These commands include "sit," "stay," "down," and "no." More difficult commands will come later. First the hunter wants to get the puppy used to listening to commands.

◀ **Obedience training helps a hunting dog be more successful and safe in the field.**

Following the hunter's commands in the field will be crucial to helping on a hunt.

Socializing is another early step in a puppy's training. The hunter introduces the puppy to other dogs. The puppy also meets new people. At first the puppy jumps and runs around new dogs and people. But soon the puppy learns to stay calm in these situations.

Next the hunter introduces the puppy to water. The puppy splashes around in a small wading pool. The hunter lets the puppy splash and have fun. Soon the puppy is leaping into lakes and streams.

The puppy also needs to get used to the scent of birds. So the hunter ties bird feathers to the end of a string. The hunter pulls the string around. The puppy chases after the feathers as if it were a game.

Once the puppy is used to the scent, the hunter tosses the feathers into the water and tall grass. The puppy quickly rushes to retrieve them.

Hunting dogs must be comfortable in the water to hunt ducks and geese. ▶

▲ Trainers sometimes use fake birds on strings to get their dogs used to tracking and chasing.

The hunter is careful not to let the puppy chew on the feathers. The goal is for the puppy to learn to find the feathers but not to eat them.

Soon the puppy is ready for a real bird. The trainer tosses a frozen pigeon into the tall grass or water. The puppy goes to retrieve it.

During all training sessions, the hunter rewards the puppy for doing a good job. This gets the puppy excited to do each task. The hunter also keeps training sessions short and fun. The hunter wants the puppy to enjoy what it's doing.

Bang! The hunter shoots a starter pistol into the air. The young dog waits at the hunter's side. A moment later, a frozen pigeon lands in front of them.

▲ **Eventually, hunters use real birds to train their dogs.**

Another hunter has tossed the pigeon from behind the dog and hunter. The dog races to retrieve the bird. The two hunters repeat the exercise. It helps the dog get used to reacting to the sound of a gunshot. After a while, the dog is ready to retrieve a bird as soon as it hears the shot.

Finally the hunter trains the dog to find and point at birds in the field. Some hunters train separate dogs to be retrievers, pointers, and flushers. Other hunters train their dogs to do two or even all three of these skills.

The hunter hides a caged bird in some tall grass. The dog sniffs around the field. It speeds up as it gets closer to finding the cage. "Whoa," the hunter says as the dog gets close to the cage. The dog pauses and looks from the tall grass to the hunter. The dog is shaking with excitement, but the hunter has trained it well. The dog does not move an inch. The hunter rewards the dog by petting it behind the ears. The dog is ready to hunt.

Rewarding dogs for good behavior helps make them want to repeat that behavior. ▶

Chapter 3

GETTING THE BIRD

In the field, one of the two hunters slowly walked forward. He was looking for the pheasant his dog was pointing at. The dog silently held its position, allowing the hunter to move closer to the bird's hiding spot.

Suddenly there was a *whump, whump, whump* of flapping wings. A pheasant burst from its cover of tall grass. The strategy had worked. The bird was close enough for the hunter to shoot at.

The hunter's shot echoed off the trees at the edge of the field. The bird seemed to freeze in midair. Then it dropped from the sky. The pheasant fell into a thicket of brambles approximately 60 feet (18 m) away.

◀ **Pheasants tend to stay in thick cover until they are flushed, or scared out.**

▲ **Dogs are trained to bite gently on downed birds to keep the meat intact.**

The Brittanys bounded after the downed bird. It would have been difficult for the hunters to find the bird in the prickly bushes. But the dogs dove through the branches. One of the dogs gently picked up the dead bird and brought it back to the hunters.

"Let," one hunter commanded. The dog released the dead pheasant. The hunter placed the bird in a pouch and petted the dog behind the ears. Then the dogs ran off again, and the group continued to hunt. They searched for more birds. The hunters spent the afternoon stomping around in the field. With their dogs' help, they each shot their **limit** of pheasants for the day.

THINK ABOUT IT

- Many people own dogs as pets, but not all dog owners use their dogs to hunt. Are there steps in a hunting dog's training that might help with training a dog to be a good pet?
- While pheasant hunting, one hunter faces one side of the field, and the second hunter faces the other direction. Why do you think this is important for the safety of each hunter?
- Hunting dogs have traits, such as their sense of smell and ability to swim, that help hunters. Are there other ways in which these features might help people?

GLOSSARY

flushers (FLUSH-urs): Flushers are hunting dogs that chase animals out of hiding. Flushers run into thickets and bushes to scare birds into flight.

game (GAME): Game is any animal being hunted. Hunting dogs help hunt game birds.

limit (LIM-it): A limit is the most of something that is allowed. Hunters have a limit of how many birds they can shoot each day.

obedience (oh-BEE-dee-ens): Obedience is the act of following directions. A handler teaches puppies obedience.

pointers (POINT-urs): Pointers are hunting dogs that indicate where birds are hiding. Brittanys are common pointers.

retrievers (ri-TREE-vurs): Retrievers are hunting dogs used to get and bring back animals that have been shot. Retrievers are able to reach places hunters may not be able to.

socializing (SOH-shuh-lyz-ing): Socializing is being around and interacting with others. Socializing teaches puppies to stay calm in new situations.

weans (WEENS): A person weans an animal when he or she feeds it food other than its mother's milk. A hunter weans the puppies at eight weeks.

TO LEARN MORE

Books

Bowman, Chris. *Labrador Retrievers.* Minneapolis, MN: Bellwether Media, 2016.

Lambert, Hines. *Hunting Quail and Pheasants.* New York: PowerKids, 2013.

Meyer, Susan. *Hunting Dogs.* New York: Rosen, 2013.

Web Sites

Visit our Web site for links about hunting dogs:
childsworld.com/links

Note to Parents, Teachers, and Librarians: We routinely verify our Web links to make sure they are safe and active sites. So encourage your readers to check them out!

SELECTED BIBLIOGRAPHY

Davis, Tom. "Pointer or Flusher for Pheasant Hunting?" *Field & Stream*. Field & Stream Network, 2016. Web. 2 Aug. 2016.

Kermicle, Rhett. "The Right Way to Teach the Here Command." *Sport Dog Brand*. Radio Systems Corporation, 2016. Web. 2 Aug. 2016.

O'Reilly, Mike. "How to Train a Pheasant Dog." *OutdoorHub*. OutdoorHub, 26 May 2011. Web. 2 Aug. 2016.

Stewart, Mike. "Retriever Training: Using Bird Feathers." *Ducks Unlimited*. Ducks Unlimited, n.d. Web. 2 Aug. 2016.

West, Bob. "First Year Tips for Training a Hunting Puppy." *Gun Dog Magazine*. Outdoor Sportsman Group, 4 May 2016. Web. 2 Aug. 2016.

INDEX

ABOUT THE AUTHOR

Allan Morey grew up on a farm in central Wisconsin, which is where his love of animals began. He has had pet pigs, chickens, rabbits, ferrets, cats, and many other animals. He now lives in Saint Paul, Minnesota, with his wife, two kids, and of course, a couple of dogs.